THE SEAL OF PROPHETS
HIS PERSONALITY AND CHARACTER

by

Hadhrat Mirza Tahir Ahmad
Khalifatul Masih IV

Text of a lecture delivered by the Head of the Ahmadiyya Muslim Jama'at on 15th October 1989 at Heathland School, Hounslow

The Seal of Prophets-His Personality and Character
By: Hadhrat Mirza Tahir Ahmad – Khalifatul Masih IV

First published in 1992
Second Revised Edition 2003
Present Edition 2008

© Islam International Publications Ltd.

Published by:
　　Islam International Publications Ltd
　　Islamabad
　　Sheephatch Lane
　　Tilford, Surrey
　　United Kingdom GU10 2AQ

Printed in UK at:
　　Raqeem Press
　　'Islamabad'
　　Tilford, Surrey GU10 2AQ

ISBN: 1 85372 727 X

The Seal of Prophets

Table of Contents

Publisher's Note 1

Chapter 1
Kalima Shahada, and Western View of Muhammad ^{SA} 4

Chapter 2
New Era of Interpretation of Islam 8

Chapter 3
Early Life & Beginning of Prophethood 14

Chapter 4
The Prophet's View on Justice 24

Chapter 5
The Prophet as a Family Man 29

Chapter 6
The Prophet's Treatment of Animals 31

Chapter 7
The Controversy over Blasphemy 33

Chapter 8
The Prophet's View on Racism 36

Index 37

Publisher's Note

On 15th October 1989, Hadhrat Mirza Tahir Ahmad, the Supreme Head of the World-wide Ahmadiyya Muslim Community, delivered the following lecture about the Holy Prophet Muhammad, may peace and blessings of Allah be upon him, entitled 'The Seal of Prophets, His Personality and Character'.

The address was delivered at Heathland School in Hounslow. Many distinguished guests including the Mayor of Hounslow and some Members of Parliament attended it.

In 1992, this address was published in the form of a booklet. By the Grace of Allah, it has now been revised and this edition is reprinted with some amendments and additions.

Please note that the name Muhammad and his titles – the Holy Prophet, the Founder of Islam – is generally followed by the symbol [sa] for the salutation "Sal-Lallaho 'Alaihi wa Sallam" meaning 'May peace and blessings of Allah be upon him'. The names of most other prophets and messengers of God are followed by the symbol [as] for "Alaiyhis-Salam" meaning 'on whom be peace'. The actual salutations have not been set out in full, in most cases, for the sake of brevity. Muslim readers should treat the full salutation as implicit.

In the revision of this text, the following people had the honour of assisting Hadhrat Khalifatul Masih IV: Chaudhary Khurshid Ahmad Sial, Munir-ud-Din Shams, Farina Qureshi and Farida Ahmad. May Allah bless them all.

May Allah make this booklet a source of enlightenment and guidance for all – Ameen.

The Publisher

THE SEAL OF PROPHETS
HIS PERSONALITY AND CHARACTER

أَشْهَدُ أَنْ لَّا اِلٰهَ اِلاَّ اللّٰهُ وَحْدَهُ لَاشَرِيْكَ لَهُ وَ أَشْهَدُ أَنَّ مُحَمَّدًا عَبْدُهُ وَ رَسُوْلُهُ. أَمَّا بَعْدُ فَأَعُوْذُ بِاللّٰهِ مِنَ الشَّيْطٰنِ الرَّجِيْمِ

﴿بِسْمِ اللّٰهِ الرَّحْمٰنِ الرَّحِيْمِ. اَلْحَمْدُ لِلّٰهِ رَبِّ الْعَالَمِيْنَ. اَلرَّحْمٰنِ الرَّحِيْمِ. مَالِكِ يَوْمِ الدِّيْنِ. اِيَّاكَ نَعْبُدُ وَاِيَّاكَ نَسْتَعِيْنُ. اِهْدِنَا الصِّرَاطَ الْمُسْتَقِيْمَ. صِرَاطَ الَّذِيْنَ أَنْعَمْتَ عَلَيْهِمْ غَيْرِ الْمَغْضُوْبِ عَلَيْهِمْ وَلَا الضَّآلِّيْنَ.﴾

قُلْ اِنَّمَآ اَنَا بَشَرٌ مِّثْلُكُمْ يُوْحٰٓى اِلَيَّ اَنَّمَآ اِلٰهُكُمْ اِلٰهٌ وَّاحِدٌ فَمَنْ كَانَ يَرْجُوْا لِقَآءَ رَبِّهٖ فَلْيَعْمَلْ عَمَلًا صَالِحًا وَّلَا يُشْرِكْ بِعِبَادَةِ رَبِّهٖٓ اَحَدًا ۝

Say, 'I am only a man like yourselves; (but) I have received the revelation that your God is only One God. So let him, who hopes to meet his Lord, do good deeds, and let him join no one in the worship of his Lord!' (Surah Al-Kahf 18 :111)

Your worship, the Mayor of Hounslow, Honourable Members of Parliament and other distinguished guests.

We consider this function a very holy occasion because of the subject to be discussed here. I am deeply honoured and overjoyed to speak to you about something I love so much.

Chapter 1

Kalima Shahada, and Western View of Muhammad [SA]

To begin with, I recited before you the *Kalima Shahada*. Then I read the opening chapter of the Holy Qur'an and a verse from a chapter called *Al-Kahf*. *Kalima Shahada*, which I recited, was the more elaborate version of the one generally known. It is in two parts; first, Allah is one, there is no God but Allah; and the other, Muhammad is His servant, a man and a Prophet. The emphasis is on man before you move on to consider him as a prophet.

It was the shorter version of the *Kalima*, لَآاِلٰهَ اِلَّااللّٰهُ مُحَمَّدٌ رَّسُوْلُ اللّٰهِ that was before Gibbon, a famous orientalist and historian, when he opined on it. Bosworth Smith writes about it in *Mohammed and Mohammedanism (Lecture II, R. Bosworth Smith; Smith, Elder & Co., 15 Waterloo Place, London, (1874)* as follows:

> "It is almost equally strange that Gibbon, who has done such full justice to Mohammed in the general result, should say at starting, 'Mohammed's religion consists of an eternal truth, and a necessary fiction – There is one God, and Mohammed is his prophet'."
> *(Page 82)*

Smith goes on to develop this by saying:

"It was, as I have endeavoured to show, no fiction to Mohammed himself or to his followers; had it been so, Mohammedanism could never have risen as it did, nor be what it is now."
(Pages 82-83)

We are grateful to Bosworth Smith for fairly presenting one excellent western attitude towards Islam, and particularly towards the Holy Founder of Islam, Prophet Muhammad, peace be upon him. He discussed the two phases of Islam's rise and fall in his lecture *Mohammed and Mohammedanism* and I quote from him:

"During the first few centuries of Mohammedanism, Christendom could not afford to criticise or explain; it could only tremble and obey. But when the Saracens had received their first check in the heart of France, the nations which had been flying before them, faced round, as a herd of cows will sometimes do when the single dog that has put them to flight is called off; and though they did not yet venture to fight, they could at least calumniate their retreating foe."
(Page 56)

Now follow the examples of calumniation as recorded by Smith; he says:

"In the romance of 'Turpin', quoted by Renan, Mohammed, the fanatical destroyer of all idolatry, is turned himself into an idol of

gold, and, under the name of Mawmet, is reported to be the object of worship at Cadiz."
(Page 57)

Then he says:

"He is Antichrist, the Man of Sin, the Little Horn, and I know not what besides; nor do I think that a single writer, with the one strange exception of the Jew Maimonides, till towards the middle of the eighteenth century, treats of him as otherwise than a rank impostor and false prophet."
(Page 61)

To build this subject further, he goes on quoting from Renan (page 224):

"The romances of Baphomet, so common in the fourteenth and fifteenth centuries, attribute any and every crime to him, just as the Athanasians did to Arius, 'He is a debauchee, a camel stealer, a Cardinal, who having failed to obtain the object of every Cardinal's ambition, invents a new religion to revenge himself on his brethren!' "
(Page 59)

"..he occupies a conspicuous place in the 'Inferno'. Dante places him in his ninth circle among the sowers of religious discord."
(Page 59)

"With the leaders of the Reformation, Mohammed, the greatest of all Reformers, meets with little sympathy, and their hatred of him, as perhaps was natural, seems to vary inversely as their knowledge. Luther doubts whether he is not worse than Leo; Melancthon believes him to be either Gog or Magog, and probably both."

(See 'Quarterly Review', Art. Islam by Deutsch, No. 254, P. 296, Mohammed and Mohemmadanism Lecture II Pages 59-60)

Chapter 2

New Era of Interpretation of Islam

Unfortunately, this sad chapter of calumny and extreme expression of hatred against the Holy Founder of Islam did not come to an end. However, we do see a change in the wind, which has brought about one of the outstanding writers on Islam from England, that is Thomas Carlyle. He ushered in a new era of an approach towards Islam. In an age darkened by hatred he was the first lark with the courage and nobility to sing the praises of Prophet Muhammad[sa], and was the first swallow to give an indication of the coming spring.

After Carlyle, things began to change but did not go on to develop into a steady trend. Instead it remained an interrupted phenomena. We see that all through the history of criticism of the Prophet Muhammad[sa], there were scholars who sank back to their past, with a Salman Rushdie being born here and there. The birth of Rushdie is not a new phenomenon in the history of religious bigotry; deeply related to ignorance, the lack of tolerance is something well-known to man.

The introduction of the great orientalist Carlyle has already been made. Now let me quote two important passages from his book *Heroes and Hero Worship*. He says:

> "Alas, such theories are very lamentable. If we would attain to knowledge of anything in God's true Creation, let us disbelieve them wholly! They are the product of an Age of Scepticism; they indicate the saddest spiritual

paralysis, and mere death-life of the souls of men: more godless theory, I think, was never promulgated in this Earth. A false man found a religion? Why, a false man cannot build a brick house! If he do not know and follow *truly* the properties of mortar, burnt clay and what else he works in, it is no house that he makes, but a rubbish-heap. It will not stand for twelve centuries, to lodge a hundred-and-eighty millions; it will fall straitway."
(Page 279)

He observes:

"The lies, which well-meaning zeal has heaped around this man, are disgraceful to ourselves only. When Pococke inquired of Grotius, Where the proof was of that story of the pigeon, trained to pick peas from Mahomet's ear, and pass for an angel dictating to him? Grotius answered that there was no proof! It is really time to dismiss all that."
(Page 279)

The one central, most important epithet in the *Kalima* is the word *Abd*, which describes the Prophet[sa] as a man and a slave; a man so true that he became the most devoted servant of his Lord. Today I have chosen to speak not on the prophesies of Prophet Muhammad, peace and blessings of Allah be upon him, but have elected to highlight his personality as a man, as a simple servant of God and as a humble person who lived all his life among his brothers, followers and enemies as a true man. In this regard I have chosen a few facets of his real life and will share them with you, for you to judge how close to humans yet how vastly different he was.

Why I said that being *Abd* was more important is because I believe that the prophecies of a Prophet are always being disputed by the enemy. At one end the Prophet is close to His God and at the other he is close to humanity. The humans cannot directly judge the authenticity of his claim of being from God, but they most certainly can judge him as a human. If as a man he is true, it is impossible for him to be a false prophet.

Again I quote Bosworth Smith, who in turn quotes Sir William Muir, in the following words:

> "Mohammed was of middle height and of a strongly built frame; his head was large, and across his ample forehead, and above finely arching eyebrows, ran a strongly marked vein, which, when he was angry, would turn black and throb visibly. His eyes were coal black and piercing in their brightness; his hair curled slightly; and a long beard, which, like other Orientals, he would stroke when in deep thought, added to the general impressiveness of his appearance. His step was quick and firm 'like that of one descending a hill'."

(Page 83)

Bosworth Smith in the 1874 edition of his book *Mohammed and Mohammedanism,* writes about his character in the following words:

> "He was a man of few words...and good faith. They called him 'Al-Amyn,' the Trusty. His tending his employer's flocks; his journeys to Syria; possibly his short-lived friendship there with Sergius or Bahira, a Nastorian Monk; his

famous vow to succour the oppressed; his employment by Khadijah in a trade venture, and his subsequent happy marriage with her, are about the only note-worthy external incidents in his early life."
(Page 75)

However in the 1986 edition of the same book, published long after his death, we see how this has been changed:

"Hitherto a man of few words, and with few friends, he was yet noble with his own small circle of truthfulness and good faith. Men called him 'Al-Amin', or the Trusty. A rich widow, named Khadija, employed him to go on some trading journeys for her to Syria. The shepherd became a camel driver, and the trust committed to him he discharged with such fidelity and prudence that Khadija offered him her hand in marriage. She some fifteen years older than he; old enough, that is, in that Eastern climate to be his mother. Yet the marriage was one of real affection and respect, and from that time to the day of her death, a period of twenty four years, Mohammed remained faithful to her, and took no second wife, though the universal custom of his countrymen would have countenanced him in so doing."
(Pages 95-96)

Describing his early life Carlyle tells us in his book:

"But, from an early age, he had been remarked as a thoughtful man. His

companions named him '*Al Amin*, The Faithful'. A man of truth and fidelity; true in what he did, in what he spake and thought. They noted that *he* always meant something. A man rather taciturn in speech; silent when there was nothing to be said; but pertinent, wise, sincere, when he did speak; always throwing light on the matter. This is the only sort of speech *worth* speaking! Through life we find him to have been regarded as an altogether solid, brotherly, genuine man. A serious, sincere character; yet amiable, cordial, companionable, jocose even; – a good laugh in him withal: there are men whose laugh is as untrue as anything about them; who cannot laugh. One hears of Mahomet's beauty: his fine sagacious honest face, brown florid complexion, beaming black eyes; – I somehow like too that vein on the brow, which swelled-up black when he was in anger".
(Pages 287-288)

Prophet Muhammad[sa] had lived among his people for forty years before he was commissioned by God as a Prophet. Even the severest critics of his character cannot put a finger on any blemish in his life up to that age. There is no dissension or disagreement among historians regarding this fact. As such the Holy Qur'an challenged those who rejected him by saying:

فَقَدْ لَبِثْتُ فِيكُمْ عُمُرًا مِّنْ قَبْلِهِ ۚ أَفَلَا تَعْقِلُونَ ۝

"Of course, I have lived among you throughout my life before this. Why don't you use your wisdom?" (Surah Yunus 10:17)

Do you not see that a man who lived forty years of blameless life suddenly cannot turn into the most wanton man on earth. He, who never spoke a lie about his fellow beings, how could he dare speak lies about his Creator, the God he loved so much!

Chapter 3

Early Life & Beginning of Prophethood

Khadija[ra] was referred to earlier as his employer. She was the rich lady who sent him on a trade mission up to Syria. He was found to be always successful in these assignments. But I believe there was another part of this trade, which was the most successful of all, but is usually omitted from being mentioned. When Khadija[ra] ultimately married him, he was a man of twenty-five, whereas she had already passed her youth and was forty years of age. Despite this age difference, when she proposed, he accepted and lived with her for another twenty-five years. After this marriage had taken place, knowing his dignity and character, Khadija[ra] offered him her entire property and gave him everything she had. The trade I mentioned as the most honourable, most wonderful and the most successful was this: having received all that wealth and property, he distributed it entirely to the destitute without keeping a penny for himself. It is also a great tribute to Khadija[ra] who, being the richest woman of Arabia, suddenly became one of its poorest, and never raised an eyebrow, living the rest of her life most faithfully with Prophet Muhammad, may peace and blessings of Allah be upon him. She was in love with the man who had not yet emerged as a prophet. However, it was not the outward charm of that man but his inward beauty, sparkling like a jewel, which she was in love with. This became evident when the Holy Founder[sa] of Islam received his first message from God. He was so completely shaken by its force that he returned home trembling as if a fever was about to take hold of him. Khadija[ra] thought he was about to fall ill and loaded him with blankets. Later, he told her about the experience he had of an angel appearing in the form of a man and commanding him to recite. He was fearful about himself, entirely shaken, he could not fathom what was happening to him. Khadija[ra], on hearing this, addressed him and said:

> I have known you for some time and I know you look after the requirements of the needy and share their miseries. You are a person who carried the burdens of those whose backs are broken under the load of afflictions. You are restoring the virtues, which have disappeared from the earth. You are kind and considerate to relations and observe the very best conduct in relationships. You are true and always have been so. How could God let you go to waste? I believe in what you have seen.

It was purity of the man within him, which convinced his wife that he was a true Prophet. As such she became the first believer in the Holy Founder[sa] of Islam and realised that it was impossible for a true man to emerge as a false prophet.

Bosworth Smith has related this incident in his own words and says:

> "Allah will not suffer thee to fall to shame. Hast thou not been loving to thy kinsfolk, kind to thy neighbours, charitable to the poor, faithful to thy word, and ever a defender of the truth?"
> *(Page 78)*

In contrast to the attitude of Khadijah[ra] the opinion of all his friends was suddenly transformed after he declared himself to be a Messenger from God. Those who used to call him *Al-Amin*, the most trustworthy, who went to him for resolving their disputes and who trusted him entirely, started blaming him as guilty of extreme falsehood. Bosworth Smith records this contradictory attitude of the Meccans, after Prophet Muhammad's[sa] pronouncement of being commissioned from God, in the following words:

> "People pointed the finger of scorn at him as he passed by: 'There goeth the son of Abdallah, who hath his converse with the heavens!' They called him a driveller, a star-gazer, a maniac-poet. His uncles sneered, and the main body of the citizens treated him with that contemptuous indifference, which must have been harder to him to bear than active persecution."
> *(Page 79)*

Then he tells us that Meccans tried persuasion and treaties, bribes and threats against Prophet Muhammad[sa]:

> "Should they array against me and put the sun on my right hand, and the moon on my left," said Mohammed, "yet while God should command me, I would not renounce my purpose."
> *(Page 80)*

"These are not the words, nor this the course of an impostor", writes Bosworth Smith.

Prophet Muhammad[sa] was a humble man in every relationship with people and was humble, of course, to God. He was humble even to those who had accepted him to be the Prophet of God. Once in Medina, after he had already been told by God that he was the Seal of Prophets, which means the very best among them, one of his companions developed an argument with someone who held in very high respect an earlier prophet by the name of Jonah^{as}. The companion of the Holy Founder^{sa} of Islam said that Muhammad^{sa} was superior, whereas the other said that Jonah^{as} was far better. When this was reported to the Holy Prophet^{sa}, he said: "Do not declare my excellence over Jonah^{as}, son of Muta, because it is against the dignity of human relationship to go on boasting about your leaders against the leaders of others. The matter of superiority of one over the other is a question to be decided by God, not something to be exulted over." That was the message given to us, unfortunately forgotten by many Muslims of today.

A similar incident happened between a Jew and a Muslim over the question of superiority between Muhammad^{sa} and Moses^{as}. The Muslim became extremely annoyed with the haughty attitude of the Jew and even slapped him. This Jew went to the Holy Prophet^{sa} and complained. The companion responsible for this was very strongly rebuked by the Holy Prophet^{sa}, who then used the same expression as used in the last incident: "Don't declare me to be better than Moses." He went on to relate the excellence of Moses^{as} and paid tribute to him by way of comforting the distress caused to the Jew's heart.

We hear of the Holy Prophet^{sa} standing the whole night, seeking forgiveness from Allah. His companions noticed that his feet became swollen because of his standing the most part of the night in prayer. They had never seen him committing a sin and believed him to be the most innocent man on earth. They asked him: "Sinless as you are, why, O Prophet of God, you seek forgiveness from Allah?" He replied: "Should I not be grateful to my God for all the favours bestowed upon me?" At another occasion when the same question about forgiveness and man's piety was being discussed, the Holy Prophet^{sa} told his companions that no human on earth would be forgiven because of good deeds. It is only Allah's Grace, which ultimately delivers humans from the bondage of sin and grants them admission into heaven. This made them wonder and one of them asked: "O Prophet of God, will you not be forgiven for your piety and good deeds?" He said: "No, not even me. I will be forgiven only by the Grace of God. Everything belongs to Him, nothing is ours. Whatever He has granted us, we use it and employ it to the best of our knowledge and abilities. Even a man with acts of piety, having spent all his life doing good deeds, will not be forgiven because of his actions. Those noble opportunities were given to him by God."

His humility knew no bounds. When sitting among his followers, ordinarily clothed, eating the same food as they did, he did not occupy a very special place. Many a time, people were mistaken as to who was the Holy Founder[sa] of Islam. Abu Bakr[ra], who later became the First Caliph of Islam, was older than he and perhaps had a longer beard, I don't know, but something in him led some strangers to address him as the Prophet of God. In a respectful attitude he would then turn to the Holy Prophet[sa] and lead them to him.

Once Umar[ra], who later became the Second Caliph of Islam, took his permission to perform Umrah; a lesser pilgrimage to Mecca than Hajj. The Holy Prophet[sa] of Islam turned to him and said: "Yes, go ahead, perform the Umrah and please do not forget me in your prayers." Such was the humility of the man, on whose prayers every Muslim depended that he was asking one of his own servants to remember him in his prayers.

All through his life he shared in every type of hardship faced by the Muslims in general. During the Battle of the Ditch he is known to have suffered hunger along with the others. When portions were allotted in digging the ditch, he was no exception and did his part of labour. Once a companion saw him in a state that overwhelmed him. He remarked: "On the day of the Battle of Al-Ahzaab, I saw the Holy Prophet[sa] carrying earth which was covering the whiteness of his abdomen". He was saying: "Without you, O Lord, we would have no guidance, nor have given any charity, nor prayed; so please bless us with tranquillity and make firm our feet when we meet our enemy. Indeed, people have oppressed us but never shall we yield if they try to bring affliction upon us because of you."

Jaabir narrates that they were digging in the days of Al-Ahzaab and came across a big rock. They told the Holy Prophet[sa] about it. When he got up, they saw a stone tied to his belly; he had not eaten anything for three days. It was an Arab custom to tie a stone like this when extremely oppressed with hunger, perhaps this helped to alleviate its pangs. In another narration of the same incident, we find that companions of the Holy Prophet[sa] had a stone each tied to their bellies, but when the Holy Prophet[sa] lifted his shirt to show them, they saw two stones tied to his belly indicating that he was suffering from hunger more than them. Jaabir[ra], on seeing this plight, could not bear it any longer. He took his permission to leave for the women's quarters, sought his wife and asked her if she had anything to eat. She said that there was a goat and some flour. He told her to slaughter the goat because he had seen the Holy Prophet[sa] in such an unbearable state.

That was the man, Prophet Muhammad, may peace and blessings of Allah be upon him, who always shared miseries with his devoted servants. There was no difference whatsoever. On the contrary, from many narrations on this subject we can believe that he suffered the most.

He was a dauntless, fearless person who never refrained from approaching danger head on. In his lifetime, he fought many defensive battles without ever waging a single offensive war.

The Seal of Prophets

He was usually found in the most dangerous areas of the battle, where the fighting would rage like mad. A narrator reports that when the Holy Prophet[sa] was sought during a battle, they would look for him in that area where combat was at its fiercest and he would always be in the midst. Once in Medina, during the dead of the night, people heard some disturbing noises. In those days attack was feared from all sides, so they saddled their horses and went on to investigate. They found the Holy Prophet[sa] already returning from that place riding an unsaddled horse. He had gone singly, in haste, without even preparing his ride. He assured them that it was nothing serious and they could all return to their homes.

Once during a journey on a very hot summer's day, he was resting under the shade of a tree. A Bedouin, who belonged to the idolaters, saw his opportunity, as the Holy Prophet[sa] was alone. He picked up the sword of Prophet Muhammad, may peace and blessings of Allah be on him, and woke him up saying tauntingly: "Who would save you from my hands?" He replied: "Allah." This short answer so overwhelmed this man that his hands trembled and the sword fell from his hand. This time the Holy Prophet[sa] picked up the sword and asked the man: "Now, who would save you from me?" The man trembling with fear could only reply: "You are a gracious and merciful person, please spare my life." The Holy Prophet[sa] said: "Woe unto you, you did not even draw a lesson; it was God Who saved me from you." This man was pardoned, of course. The Holy Prophet[sa] was a very big-hearted person.

The Holy Prophet[sa] loved no place on earth greater than a mosque. This love in his heart was so intense that it is inconceivable for anyone else to have similar feelings. Once a Bedouin who was not a Muslim came to visit Medina and was lodged in the mosque. In those days and even today in some parts of the world, mosques are used as guesthouses. Being a place of worship, mosques are kept very clean, even shoes are not permitted inside. But this man, out of ignorance, started urinating in the courtyard of the mosque. The Holy Prophet[sa] and his companions were present in the mosque at that time. Some of the companions rushed towards him to punish him for this offence, but were immediately stopped by the Holy Prophet[sa]. They were told not to disturb him during the act. When he had finished the Holy Prophet[sa] asked for a bucket of water and he himself washed that place. Then he turned to his companions and said: "You were not raised by God to cause difficulties for people. Always remember that you were raised to bring relief to mankind".

Once a delegation of Christian leaders from Najraan came to Medina for debating issues of difference between Islam and Christianity. They stayed there for three days. While engaged in a dialogue in the Holy Prophet's[sa] mosque, the time for their prayers arrived. They asked permission from the Holy Prophet[sa] to go out to offer their prayers. The Holy Prophet, may peace and blessings of Allah be upon him, said that the mosque was also a place of worship and they were welcome to pray there, and they did. In the meantime, some companions reached the mosque and saw the Christians worshipping facing the opposite direction from the Qiblah in that Mosque. They moved forward to object to this, but he firmly prohibited them from interfering and said: "I have permitted them because this is the house of God, and no man has the right to object to anyone who worships God in a place devoted for the sake of worship".

On another occasion, a delegation from the monastery of St Catherine begged him to write a pronouncement to the effect that their monastery should be protected when Islam would become victorious in that part of the world. The Holy Prophet[sa] immediately accepted the request and wrote orders to that effect. To my knowledge, the parchment on which this order was written is still preserved in Turkey. It reads: 'No one should ever interfere with the property of the Monastery, nor with the figure of the cross or any other article which represents their faith. They should not be molested in any manner whatsoever. Anyone ignoring this will not be one of us'.

So much is said about the prevailing hatred between Muslims and Jews but it was just one-sided during the time of the Holy Prophet[sa]. Although the Jewish clans in and around Medina vehemently opposed Prophet Muhammad[sa], his conduct to them always remained just and humane. Once when he was sitting with his companions, a funeral procession passed nearby and he stood up in respect. Someone pointed out that the corpse belonged to a Jew. He replied: "Was this person not given life by God? Was he not a creation of God? Remember, in things which are common to man, we must show respect, irrespective of one's religion, race or creed". This is the essence of Islam, it was not only taught by word of mouth but was also practised in every detail.

He was a man of love, a love of beauty mingled with humility. He loved children, even respected them. After the demise of the Holy Prophet[sa], one of his companions passed through a group of children and said *Assalam-o-Alaikum* (peace be on you). They were young and were surprised that a highly respected elderly person, a companion of the Holy Founder[sa], was greeting them by saying: "Peace be on you." When he found the children so surprised, he told them: "I always observed the Holy Founder[sa] doing this. It was his habit to take the lead in saying *Assalam-o-Alaikum* even to children".

Osamah bin Zaid[ra] narrates that while he was a child he was picked up by the Holy Prophet[sa] and put on one of his knees, then the Holy Prophet[sa] put his grandson Hasan[ra] on his other knee, and embracing them both prayed to God: "Oh my Lord, show mercy to them as I am showing mercy to them". This incident left an indelible mark on Osamah bin Zaid[ra], who reported it with tears in his eyes.

The Holy Founder[sa] of Islam had a very pleasant sense of humour. He used to joke with children to amuse them with light talk. However his humour would never hurt anyone. There are many reports of his jokes with children and sometimes with old people.

Anas[ra] reports: The Holy Prophet[sa] used to become intimate with children. Once my younger brother's sparrow called "Nughar" died. The Holy Prophet[sa] cheered him up by saying: 'O Abu Omair! What has little Nughar (calling it as 'Nughair') done to you?' Whenever he met him, he said the same thing until Abu Omair forgot his Nughar and started enjoying being addressed by the Holy Prophet[sa] thus.

Once Hasan[ra], the grandson of the Holy Prophet[sa] wanted to ride a camel. He seated him on his shoulders and posed to be his camel. This made Hadhrat Hasan[ra] smile with pleasure. All such small jokes are not reported, but this much is certainly reported that he always had similar pleasing talks with small children.

Once an old woman enquired from him whether she would also be granted permission to enter paradise. In answer the Holy Prophet[sa] said that no old person would ever enter paradise. She was deeply taken aback at that and expressed her grief. The Holy Prophet[sa] smilingly put her at ease by observing: All those who enter the paradise would have been turned young.

Chapter 4

The Prophet's View on Justice

The Holy Prophet[sa] was a man of strict and absolute justice. However, his justice was complemented with a balancing sense of perfect kindness. In the Battle of Badr, one of his uncles Abbas, while fighting on the side of the idolaters, was arrested by the Muslims. Like other prisoners, his hands and feet were also bound against a pillar in the mosque, but rather too tight. The Holy Prophet[sa], whose home was adjacent to the mosque, could not sleep at night, distressed at hearing his sobs and cries. When this was reported to his companions present in the mosque, they loosened Abbas's ties. After a while, when the Holy Prophet[sa] couldn't hear any moaning, he became worried and enquired as to why the sounds had stopped. Somebody said that the ties of Abbas had been relaxed. He said: "If you have done this to Abbas do the same to every prisoner". This having been done he could at least rest in peace. This is how he showed his kindness without compromising justice.

Once a daughter of a prominent Arab chieftain was caught stealing; her name was Fatimah, the same as that of the Holy Prophet's[sa] daughter. This matter was being disputed outside the house of the Holy Prophet[sa] and some people were asking for mercy as she was the daughter of a powerful chief. They persuaded Osamah[ra], the son of a liberated slave of the Holy Prophet[sa], whom the Holy Prophet[sa] loved so much, to intercede on her behalf. He proceeded to do so. But this annoyed the Holy Prophet[sa] so much that the vein on his forehead darkened and he said: "What do you mean by this intercession? I would most certainly have done what Allah wants me to do even if my daughter Fatimah[ra] had committed this crime".

The Holy Prophet[sa] once owed money to a Jew. The Jew thought it was overdue whereas it was not so. He confronted the Holy Prophet[sa] and demanded his money, using very harsh words, and accused that all Quraish were bad debtors who never honoured their promises. He had not only insulted the Holy Prophet[sa] but also his tribe. Umar[ra], who was also there, became extremely annoyed and his hand went for his sword. The Holy Prophet[sa] stopped Umar[ra], who had now used some abusive words against the Jew and was perhaps about to strike him, and said: "Umar, you should have behaved differently. First you should have told me to be mindful of the contract and pay in time, then you should have told him to be kind in his demands and merciful to his debtors". Then he turned to another of his companions and said: "Still there are three days, I know the limit is not yet over, but pay him whatever I owe and add some more because of the harsh attitude of Umar". This was his behaviour when openly insulted in the company of his companions. His sense of justice was supreme. It was absolute, not in any way connected to his personal, tribal or religious loyalties.

Today the Jewish/Muslim relationship is a much-misunderstood concept and needs to be corrected. I will quote some examples from the Holy Prophet's[sa] relationship with Jews because we must follow his conduct in this regard; any contradictory attitude has to be dismissed. The Holy Founder of Islam, may peace and blessings of Allah be upon him, had built an image in the society of being a man of absolute justice. Even when there were feuds between Muslims and Jews, or Muslims and idolaters, they would seek his judgement. In one case it is reported that a piece of land was disputed between a Muslim and a Jew. They approached the Holy Prophet[sa] and asked him to decide the matter. The Holy Prophet[sa] first asked the Muslim claimant to provide proof. The Muslim said that he had no witnesses but was telling the truth on his word of honour. The Holy Prophet[sa] ignored him and asked the respondent to swear in the name of God if the land belonged to him. The Muslim protested and said: "O Prophet of God, he will swear falsely. It is trivial for him to be untruthful for a piece of land". The Holy Prophet[sa] replied: "There is no other way to decide this matter, if he swears then the land would be his". And that is exactly what happened.

Once a small trade party visited Khaiber, an area occupied by a Jewish clan by the name of Bani-Nazeer. These people were earlier expelled from Medina and were rehabilitated there; but that is a different story. This place had become a Jewish stronghold from then on. When the trade party from among the Muslims visited Khaiber, one of them was murdered. They returned to the Holy Prophet[sa] and asked that the responsibility for the murder should be placed on Jews of that area, and blood money imposed on them as a group. The Holy Prophet[sa] said: "Do you have any proof of this man being murdered by a Jew?" They replied: "There is no witness but it has to be one of them, nobody else lives there." The Holy Prophet[sa] said: "The only available course is that the Jews must swear their innocence." The Jews did that and were acquitted of the murder. However, by the order of the Holy Prophet[sa], the aggrieved were paid blood money from the state treasury. We see in him kindness wedded to his sense of justice in the most beautiful and well poised way, which is indeed a pleasure to watch.

The Holy Prophet[sa] was also very kind to his servants and slaves. The question of slavery is a much-misunderstood concept in the West. I will not touch upon this in any detail but I assure you that there is only one permissible way mentioned in the Holy Qur'an, by which slaves can be en-slaved. This is in Chapter Al-Anfaal, verse sixty-eight. It reads that the only way of making human beings slaves is after a very severe battle, not just a skirmish. In those days there was no system of prisoner of war camps, so the prisoners would be distributed to different homes. We also see that the Holy Qur'an goes on to suggest numerous routes for liberation of the slaves. There are so many verses on this subject, that after going through these, it is surprising how slavery could ever be conceived by the present day Muslims as validated perpetually. According to the Holy Qur'an, if a slave is not liberated by ransom paid by his relatives, and has no other means of getting liberated, he can demand his liberation from a Muslim court. All he has to do is to appeal to the court, asking immediate release, on the condition that he will earn and pay back on small easy instalments whatever cost is considered to be his value. These injunctions were very strictly imposed in the days of the Holy Prophet[sa]. Sometimes thousands of slaves were liberated in a single day. Owing to the legacy of the past and also because those were troubled times, some slaves were inherited by people and went on serving private homes. The Holy Prophet[sa] repeatedly admonished Muslims that they should be as kind to them as to their kith and kin. We find mention of many such incidents; for instance, when a master and a slave went together for buying something, the shopkeepers could not distinguish between them as to who was the master and who was the slave. Once Ali[ra], who later became the Fourth Caliph of Islam, after the Holy Prophet[sa], went shopping and asked for two identical pieces of clothing. The shopkeeper suggested that he should buy clothes of different colour. He said: "My master, may peace and blessings of Allah be upon him, told me to treat my slaves as I would my own kith and kin. So whatever I wear, I shall make my slave wear the same".

Abu Masood Badri[ra] relates: "I was striking a slave with a whip when I heard a voice behind me: "Beware, Abu Masood". I was so upset that I did not recognise the voice until the person drew near and I discovered it was the Holy Prophet[sa] and he was saying: "Beware, Abu Masood. Allah has more power over you than you have over this slave", and I responded: "Messenger of Allah, I will set him free to win the pleasure of Allah". The Holy Prophet[sa] observed: "If you had not done that you would have been singed by the fire".

Zaid[ra] is often quoted in the history of Islam because he is the only slave to have lived with the Holy Founder[sa] of Islam. He reports: "During my service to the Holy Prophet[sa], I made many mistakes, but he never said woe to me, even once. He never criticised me. There was no question of beating me of course."

Zaid[ra] was bought as a slave by Muhammad (before his prophethood) during the pre-Islamic period. Zaid's father and uncle who lived in Persia, came to learn that Zaid[ra] could be found in Mecca serving as a slave to (Hadhrat) Muhammad (may peace and blessings of Allah be upon him). They approached him in Mecca and begged him to liberate Zaid[ra]. He said: "Of course I will do that but why not ask him? He is a free man; if he wants to stay I cannot compel him to leave." So he kept quiet while Zaid[ra] was made to appear before his father and uncle. There was an emotional meeting as they had met after a long time. They asked Zaid[ra] to return to his home. He replied: "If the choice is mine, I will not return because I have discovered a man who is dearer to me than my father, my mother, my uncle and everyone else in the world." Hearing this, the Holy Founder[sa] of Islam took them out and, in the presence of some people proclaimed: "I declare that Zaid[ra] is no longer a slave. From now on he will be my adopted son."

Chapter 5

The Prophet as a Family Man

Now I will turn to another aspect of the Holy Prophet Muhammad^{sa}, as a father, as a husband, and as a man in relation to his other relatives. Hadhrat Aishah^{ra} reports that whenever the Holy Prophet's^{sa} daughter Fatimah^{ra} visited him, he always stood up showing respect for her, kissed her hand and had her seated where he himself had been seated.

He always treated with kindness and respect the relatives of his late wife Khadijah^{ra}, extending the same to her friends. Likewise he treated the relatives of his wet-nurse Halimah. Once a close relative of hers visited the Prophet^{sa}. He stood up and spread a sheet for her to sit upon. When enquired about her, she was introduced by him as a close relative to his wet-nurse whom he respected like he would respect his own mother.

In relation to his wives, although there are reports of Aishah^{ra} and his other wives losing their temper with him, never once is he reported to have retorted in the same way. He is never known to have addressed them harshly.

Aishah^{ra} narrates that he helped her in the daily household chores, all this over and above his duties to the whole of mankind as a Prophet of God. He mended his own clothes and shoes, went himself to fetch water for his use and would never seek help in these matters. This aspect of his character impressed his companions immensely.

Aishah^{ra} describes his bedding as a sack of hide filled with leaves. She says: " We never ate bread made of wheat for three consecutive days. There were times when months would pass and we did not eat meat or bread, instead filled our bellies with dates and some milk, except for an odd present when someone would slaughter a sheep and send us a piece of meat." Umar narrates: "I went into a small room which was occupied by the Holy Founder[sa] of Islam. He was lying on a straw bedding so rough in nature that on the side he was leaning, I saw straw marks all over his body. I scanned the room and it was empty, there was nothing except for a small bucket for water and one or two odd things. I knew him to be the most beloved of God, a person who had reached the summit of humanity. This contrast so overwhelmed me with sorrow that I started to cry." The Holy Prophet[sa] turned to me and said: "Umar, what has ailed thee?" I said: "O Messenger of God, God loves you so much, you are the best ever created by Him, yet I see you in this state of extreme austerity. You don't have proper bedding, you don't have any articles to decorate your house, there is nothing." The Holy Prophet[sa] smiled and said: "Umar, would you prefer worldly things of this life to what is in store for us by God in the life to come?" Umar[ra] replied: "Surely the things to come will be better".

This is a small incident, but could an impostor do this? Why do people concoct lies? For what purpose? Is it to live such lives of austerity and pain, and for sharing miseries of their time with their devoted servants? If that is a lie, then there is no sense in truth itself; everything in man has to be false.

Chapter 6

The Prophet's Treatment of Animals

The Holy Prophet[sa] was extremely kind even to animals. Once on a journey, he heard cries of a small bird in distress. He turned to his companions and asked what had happened to the bird. One of them said that he had taken two eggs from her nest. The Holy Prophet[sa] said: "Return them immediately." In another narration of the same incident it is said that two chicks and not eggs had been taken, and the Holy Prophet[sa] said to his companions that no mother should ever be pained on account of her offspring.

The Holy Prophet[sa] once narrated an incident to his companions: "A man who was thirsty in a desert discovered a well full of water. He climbed down and drank his fill. Upon coming out, he observed a dog panting with thirst, perhaps about to die. He went back in and filled his shoes with water, then holding them in his teeth, returned to the surface and quenched the thirst of the dog. The Holy Founder[sa] said: "God has told me that this man was pardoned for all his previous sins." In another narration it is said that it was a prostitute who did this. Her whole life was full of sins, but she was pardoned in the sight of God for an act of kindness to an animal.

One of his companions asked if they would be rewarded for acts of mercy to animals. He said: "Yes, all those animals who have wet livers." The word 'wet' in Arabic is used to indicate softness and sensibility. I have translated it literally but the connotation is that any animal with sensibility and sensitivity to pain is to be treated kindly, and God would reward for all such acts of kindness.

Once the Holy Prophet[sa] saw someone milking a goat and was worried if any milk was left for its kids. He admonished the man to always leave enough milk for the hungry kids.

He prohibited his companions from killing any bird or animal, just for the sake of killing. He said: "You will be answerable to God for killing purposelessly and without justification." When asked what would be the justification, he said: "You may only kill animals when you need their meat". He then reminded them that even in killing they must not be bereft of mercy: "Kill in a manner that the animal feels least pain."

Some people ask me if the modern style of slaughtering is Islamic, which is first stunning the animal, and then slaughtering it. In answer I say that it is not un-Islamic. I do not agree with orthodox Muslim scholars who say that this system was unknown to early Islam. These instruments which help alleviate the pain of animals were not available in those days. However, the principle, that even in killing you should show mercy, was enunciated by the Holy Founder[sa] of Islam himself.

Chapter 7

The Controversy over Blasphemy

Now I turn to the most hotly debated question of today, that of blasphemy. Wherever I visit in the world, this question pursues me. I am asked about Khomeini's edict of death against Salman Rushdie. I tell them the Islam I learned from the Holy Prophet[sa], speaks of no punishment whatsoever against blasphemy. No question of death or anything else for that matter. Among other things, I quote this particular incident in the life of the Holy Prophet[sa], also briefly recorded in the Holy Qur'an. Before the Holy Prophet's[sa] arrival in Medina, there was a prominent leader who by the consensus of Medinite, was rising to be their joint leader. His name was Abdullah Bin Obey Bin Salul. After the Prophet's[sa] arrival things gradually changed and instead of Abdullah, the Holy Prophet[sa] was accepted by the common consensus of people as their new leader. This made Abdullah Bin Obey Bin Salul extremely jealous. He went on giving voice to his injured feelings in one way or another. His behaviour was such that the other Muslims referred to him as the chief *monaafiq*, meaning the chief of hypocrites. Once, when returning from an expedition which was overall a failure, and all participants were extremely tired and disappointed, this man Abdullah, thought it a fit time to take his revenge. In the presence of a few people, he declared that upon returning to Medina, the noblest among them would turn out in disgrace the meanest of them. The message was clear and everyone knew what he meant. Umar[ra], upon hearing this, asked permission of the Holy Prophet[sa] to kill this man; he said that the insult on the person of the Holy Prophet[sa] was far too much for them to tolerate. But the Holy Prophet[sa] did not allow any retribution. It is reported that after this, Abdullah's own son also approached the Holy Prophet[sa] and said: "Oh Messenger of God, perhaps you thought that if you had permitted someone else to kill my father, I being his son, may harbour a private sense of revenge. However my father deserves this punishment for the insult he has hurled against you, so please permit me to slay him." The Holy Prophet[sa] smiled and said: "No, there is nothing to be done. Your father will not be punished by any one."

They all returned to Medina and for many years this man lived in peace under the full protection of the Holy Founder[sa] of Islam, against whom he had blasphemed. When he died, the Holy Prophet[sa] decided to lead his funeral prayers. This was a bit too much for some of his companions. Umar[ra] reports that he blocked his passage and said: "Is he not the leader of the hypocrites? Is he not the one about whom God has said that even if you ask forgiveness for him seventy times, he would not be forgiven? Then why O Prophet of God, who is the recipient of all these revelations, have you decided to lead his funeral prayer?" The answer was: "Umar, get aside; if God has informed me that he would not forgive the hypocrites even if I prayed for them seventy times, I would pray much more than that in the hope that Allah will ultimately forgive them". Such was the character of the Holy Founder[sa] of Islam. He was a man of extreme compassion, a man of principles, a man who lived a life of truth and nothing but the truth.

When he found that the days of return to his Holy Master, Allah were nigh, the Holy Prophet[sa] addressed a large gathering. It was the largest gathering that he had ever spoken to. The occasion was of the last pilgrimage, also called Hajja-tul-Widaa. During that sermon, his message was to all mankind and for all times to come. He addressed them as "mankind" and not as "Muslims". He said: "O mankind! All of you are equal. There is no preference to an Arab over a non-Arab, no preference to a white man over a black. All men, whatever nation or tribe they belong to, and whatever station in life they may hold, are equal. The only preference that can be conceived is one's fear of God." At the end he said: "Tell me if I have delivered the message." They all said in one voice: "Yes, O Prophet of God, you have surely delivered the message." He said: "Now promise me, you will go on spreading this message to the whole of mankind, to the corners of the earth. Whoever is present must go on delivering the message to those who are absent and this should go on till the end of time."

Chapter 8

The Prophet's View on Racism

Racism is another hotly debated question. Though many civilised nations would deny its undercurrents, my experience suggests that it is found in every people and in every part of the world. It is not just a question of white feeling a kind of superiority over the black, but also the black nurture a feeling of vindictive superiority over the white. It remains the most dangerous undercurrent of human thought and motivation. Under the explicit instructions of the Holy Prophet[sa], I deliver to you this message of racial equality. All of us being the creation of God, belonging to the same ancestry, how can we permit ourselves to sink to the level where issues of human superiority over others take grip of us.

When the time of his departure from this life was near, the Holy Prophet[sa] was given a choice by God to either return to Him or spend some more years in this earthly existence. His answer was: *"Fir-Rafiqil-A'ala*: I prefer to return to my Exalted Lord." These were the last words he uttered before passing on to eternal life.

This is the man called Muhammad[sa]. His reality has been long distorted by the unreal legends built by his adversaries. It is high time that the West and the whole world following it, stop believing blindfolded in the legends and return to the reality. The reality of Muhammad[sa] is far from being hate worthy. His reality is only to be loved and is always to be loved till the end of mankind.

Index

Abbas 24
Abd 9, 10
Abdullah 33
Abdullah Bin Obey Bin Salul 33
Abu Bakr[ra]
   First Caliph of Islam 18
Abu Masood Badri[ra] 27
Aishah[ra] 29
Al Amin
   Title given to Holy Prophet[sa] for his truth and fidelity 11
Ali[ra]
   Fourth Caliph of Islam 27
Allah the Almighty
   Unity affirmed in *Kalima Shahada* 4
Animals
   Holy Prophet's[sa] kindness to 31
   Humane slaughter 32
   Killing of 32
Assalam-o-Alaikum 22
   Bani-Nazeer 26
Baphomet
   malicious comments regarding Holy Prophet[sa] 6, 7
Battle of Al-Ahzaab
   Holy Prophet's[sa] Suffering ... 19
   Holy Prophet[sa]'s prayer during 19
Battle of Badr 24
Battle of the Ditch
   Sufferings during 18
Blasphemy 33, 37
Bosworth Smith .... *See* Smith, Bosworth
Carlyle, Thomas
   on Holy Prophet's[sa] early life 11
   Quotations from 8
   Views of, about Holy Prophet[sa]
   .... 8, 9
Christendom 5
Dante
   calumny of 6
Equality
   Message in Farewell Pilgrimage 36
Farewell Pilgrimage .. See Hajja-tul-Widaa
Fatimah[ra]
   Daughter of Prophet 24, 29
Forgiveness
   Depends on Grace of Allah .. 18
Gibbon
   Orientalist & Historian 4
Grotius 9
Hajja-tul-Widaa
   Holy Prophet's[sa] message on. 34
Halimah 29
Hasan[ra]
   Love of Holy Prophet[sa] for, ... 22, 23
Holy Prophet's[sa] mosque
   Christians permitted to pray in, ... 21
Holy Prophet[sa]
   Absolute Justice 24, 25, 26
   as Shepard & Camel driver ... 11
   Change in the attitude of friends after Prophethood . 16
   Characteristics 22, 23
   Companions's testimony of sinlessness 17
   Compassion of 21
   Courage of 20
   Distribution of wealth after marriage 14
   Greatest of all reformers 6
   Humanity of, affirmed in

37

Index

Kalima Shahada 4
Humility 16, 17
Humility of 18, 19
Last words of 36
Love for children. 22, 23
Love for mosques 20
Physical description 10, 11
Prohibiting his companions to boast of his superiority over prophets 16, 17
Receives first message from Allah 14, 15
Respect for funeral 22
Seal of Prophets 16
Seeking forgiveness of Allah 17
Sense of humour 23
Simple life of 29, 30
Title of Al-Amin 10, 12, 15
treatment of wives 29
Trust in Allah 20
Unfair critics of 5
Holy Quran
on Holy Prophet's[sa] blameless life 12
Jaabir[ra] 19
Jew 25
Debate of a Muslim with 17
Jewish/Muslim relations
misunderstandings about 25
Jews
Opposed Holy Prophet[sa] 22
Justice
Procedure for evidence 24, 25, 26
Kalima Shahada
meaning of 4
Khadijah[ra]
Employment of Holy Prophet[sa] 11, 16
Holy Prophet's[sa] treatment of relatives of 29
Marriage with Holy Prophet[sa] 14
Sacrifices made by 14
Statement regarding Holy Prophet's[sa] character 15
Khaiber 26
Khomeini 33
Luther
Calumny of 7
Maimonides
on Holy Prophet[sa] 6
Meccans
Opposition of Holy Prophet[sa] 16
Threats against Holy Prophet[sa] 16
Medina .16, 20, 21, 22, 26, 33, 34
Medinite .... See Medina
Melancthon
Calumny of 7
Monaafiq 33
Monastery of St Catherine
Prnouncement given to ... 21, 22
Muir, Sir William
on Holy Prophet's[sa] physical description 10
Osamah bin Zaid[ra]
Love of Holy Prophet[sa] for ... 22
Persia 28
Pococke 9
Prophecies
of a prophet, always disputed 10
Prophethood: 14, 28
Racism 36
Racial equality 36
Renan
Distorted portrait of Islam .. 5, 6
Salman Rushdie
Khomeini's edict of death 33
Product of bigotry 8
Slavery
abolition of 26, 27
Slaves
Liberation of 27

Treatment of 26, 27
Smith, Bosworth
   Comments regarding Holy
     Prophet's[sa] character 10
   Critique of Gibbon's views
     regarding Holy Prophet[sa] 4
   Excellent attitude towards
     Islam 5
   on calumniation of Islam 5
   on contradictions of the
     Meccan's 16
   on Khadija's testimony 15
   on truthfulness of Holy
     Prophet[sa] 16

Pivotal changes in the book of
   11
Thomas Carlyle ...... *See* **Carlyle, Thomas**
Truthfulness
   The only criterion to Judge a
     Prophet 10
Umar[ra] **18, 30, 33, 34, 35**
   Second Caliph of Islam 18
Zaid[ra]
   History of 28
   on the kindness of Holy
     Prophet[sa] 22, 28